"I had a lot of dates but I decided to stay home and dye my eyebrows."

Andy Warhol

SINGLE: THE PLEASURES OF LIVING SOLO

© IMP AB 2006

CREATIVE TEAM
Helen Svensson: producer/idea/art direction/graphic design
Lehna Edwall: idea/set design/re:construction
Christian Callert/lovechild: idea/copy
Tomas Svensson/lovechild: idea/art direction/typography
Erik Olsson: photography

Lotta Mossum: assistant re:construction
Tomas Ökvist: graphic design
Staffan Daun: image control
WriteRight: translation

Rotolito Lombarda SpA
Printed in Italy 2006
ISBN 10: 91-7002-533-9
ISBN 13: 978-91-7002-533-4

SINGLE

The pleasures of living solo

On hearing that someone is single, people often say, "How sad", or "What's wrong with them?". It's enough to make a single person want to jump up and add, "Only for the short term". Because if you say that you are single and like it that way, you risk simply not being believed.

We are here to challenge that prejudice! Consider some of the fantastic aspects of living solo: you don't have to ask anyone before you paint the ceiling pink; you don't have to put up with somebody else's collection of Star Wars memorabilia; or engage in a constant battle about whether the toilet seat should be up or down.

In short, the big advantage of being single is that you are *free*. Free to please yourself. Free to find your own style and put your own stamp on your home. Free to explore who you are and make your home your castle.

This is exactly what the owners of the homes featured here have done. *So come in and be inspired!*

After years of minimalism, discover maximalism. These 25 m² belong to a woman in a creative profession who is accustomed to thinking differently in the face of a challenge. Like living large without lots of room. Like mixing colours, textures, books and knick-knacks without making the place look cluttered. Welcome to a home packed with creativity.

MEET THE MAXIMALIST ☛

...they this they —
a Catologue.
Gertrude Stein

FIRST IMPRESSIONS. The hall is a tricky place for most of us. Even if we just have ourselves to take care of, clothes and shoes have a tendency to pile up all over the place. In this hall, however, the clutter is hidden away thanks to clever use of all the available wall space. But to keep the place shipshape, there is really no alternative to frequent tidying up.

POST-IT® XXL. Posting large to-do notes on your wall is a decorative way of organizing your life.

SPARE US THE CLUTTER. If only we could live like the Buddhist monks, with only three possessions. It seems living inevitably results in ever-growing piles of things. In this home, things like books, CDs and magazines are arranged to become interior design instead of clutter.

THREE WORDS TO GET MORE COLOUR INTO YOUR HOME: DARE, DARE, DARE.

THE LEAN CUISINE. Yes, it's all there: kitchen sink, oven, fridge and plenty of room for all the utensils you want to use but not put on show. There is even room for the computer.

WORKSTATION

When space is limited, but expectations are limitless, you have to think harder. *Organization is the key.* Prioritize. Boxes can hide the things you rarely need, while those items in frequent use can be arranged for easy accessibility.

UNITED COLOURS. Artists have long known surrounding colours affect the way a colour looks. Pinning up paper of different colours is an attractive way of exploring this.

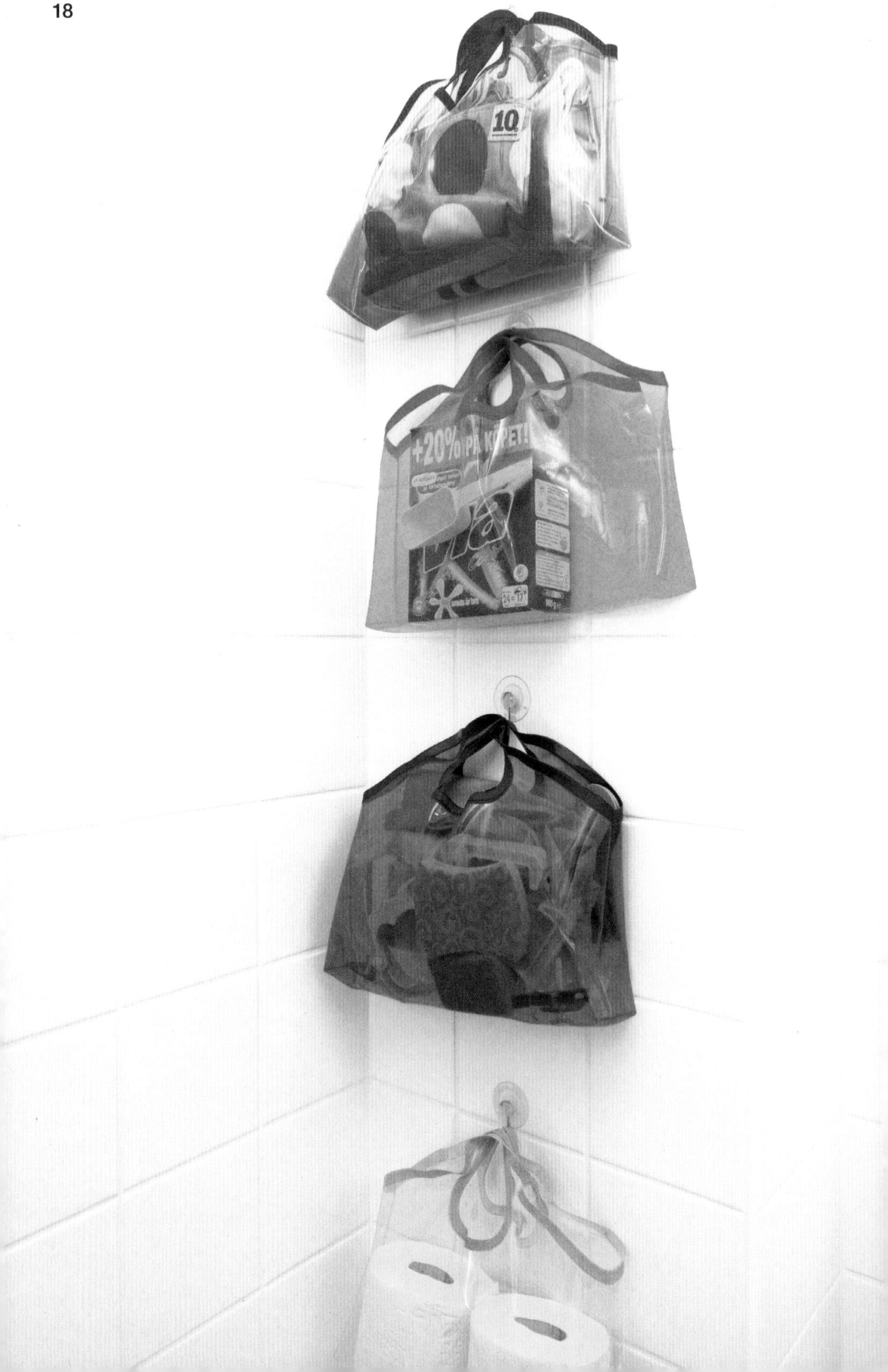
10
+20%

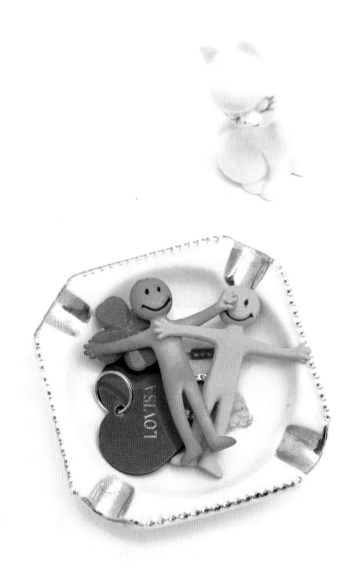

One universal trick almost always works when decorating a home: surround yourself with the things you love. Regard them as different aspects of yourself, and they will blend and coalesce.

re:construction#1. Many inventors have used the trick of combining words randomly to open their minds to new thoughts. It is said this technique was how the refrigerator was invented. Maybe this rockable bathtub was invented in the same way. It's an old tub and second-hand tyres painted a warm yellow. The idea is to rock away your stresses and strains in a lovely hot bath. And since it is portable, you can put it wherever you like.

WHIRLPOOL

re:construction

Behind this book is a team of people experienced in archi-
tecture, set design, styling, advertising and design.

We have allowed ourselves the pleasure of playing
around with some familiar and some less familiar common
products. We wanted to show how easy it is to devise fantastic new things out of ordinary ones. But there's more to
it than fun. We hope to challenge your way of looking at interior design, to get you to experiment more and to expand
your imagination. We call these experiments "re:construc-
tions", and you will find them scattered among the pages.

The first, a wall of buckets, demonstrates the three
watchwords that have guided us: fun, cheap and useful.

re:construction#2

Plastic buckets are cheap and useful. If you are lucky enough to have a larder, try attaching loads of buckets to one of the walls. Voilà! You will have created handy storage containers for a very small investment. Of course buckets offer solutions in other places as well. In the garage for tools and stuff, in the entryway for clothes and shoes, in the cupboard for towels or whatever. You can make a system of different coloured buckets for sorting laundry.

BUCKET BRIGADE

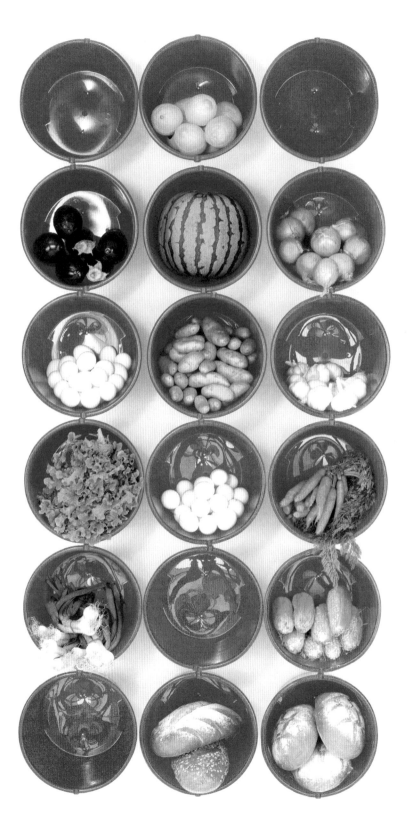

re:construction#3

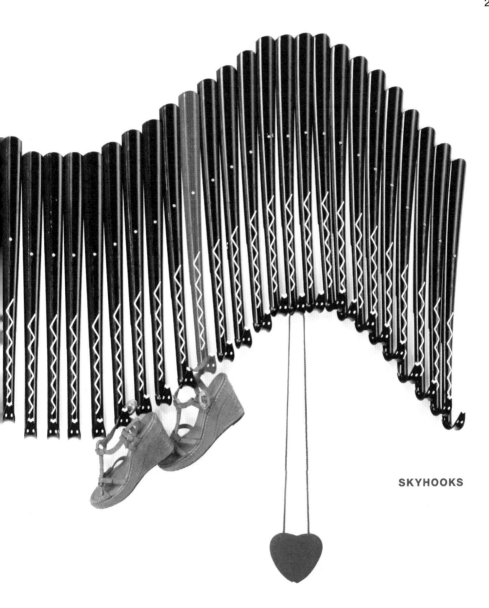

SKYHOOKS

A cheap thing is simply that: a cheap thing. But a bunch of cheap things combined turns into something precious. These shoehorns, nailed close together on a wall, have metamorphosed into a wave of hooks.

Frustrated that, as a boy, his friends had more Star Wars toys than him, this resident set out to prove success is the sweetest revenge and built his own private empire. He methodically purchased every Star Wars item he could lay his hands on, first from the aforementioned friends, then by advertising in local magazines and by bidding at web auctions. He is the proud owner of a very, very large collection in his four-room

flat. The gems, of course, are items in original pack-
aging from the first Star Wars series in 1977–85. To
avoid the risk of living in a museum, some of the toys
are used as part of the interior decor. With this assem-
blage, life can be neither boring nor lonely. And, since
Star Wars keeps engaging people all over the world,
the collection will never stop growing.

THE COLLECTOR ☞

IT'S IN OUR DNA. Archaeological finds dating back 120,000 years show that our ancestors were collectors. Though gathering food was their main priority, there is also evidence that they collected items they thought were decorative, such as stones and pieces of wood.

HOME THEATRE

JABBA THE SHOT

COMMERCIAL SPACE: The serious collector must of course have somewhere to display his treasures. Exclusive business deals take place in this room, dollars change hands and Boba Fett gets a new home while the cantina band plays Benny Goodman in the background. It's a serious business playing with dolls.

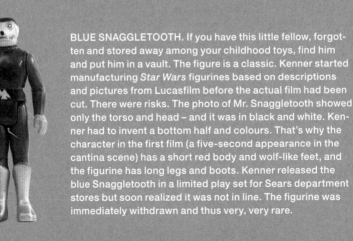

BLUE SNAGGLETOOTH. If you have this little fellow, forgotten and stored away among your childhood toys, find him and put him in a vault. The figure is a classic. Kenner started manufacturing *Star Wars* figurines based on descriptions and pictures from Lucasfilm before the actual film had been cut. There were risks. The photo of Mr. Snaggletooth showed only the torso and head – and it was in black and white. Kenner had to invent a bottom half and colours. That's why the character in the first film (a five-second appearance in the cantina scene) has a short red body and wolf-like feet, and the figurine has long legs and boots. Kenner released the blue Snaggletooth in a limited play set for Sears department stores but soon realized it was not in line. The figurine was immediately withdrawn and thus very, very rare.

PRIVATE SPACE

re:construction#4

In the early 1960s, legendary record producer Phil Spector invented a revolutionary music production technique that used layer on layer of instruments to create the effect of a wall of sound. Among the many examples of his wall of sound performers are the Ronettes, the Crystals and the Righteous Brothers. Create your own wall of sound. Just pick your favourite artists and carefully mount them to a wall, instead of hiding them in racks or shelves.

WALL OF SOUND

The CD cases are mounted to the wall using double-sided foam adhesive tape. The tape is thick, so you can safely open the CD cases. And don't worry, it sticks!

Top ten singles

The best selling singles in the UK of all times.

1 Something About The Way You Look Tonight /
Candle In The Wind 1997
Elton John
2 Do They Know It's Christmas?
Band Aid
3 Bohemian Rhapsody
Queen
4 Mull Of Kintyre / Girls School
Wings
5 Rivers Of Babylon / Brown Girl In The Ring
Boney M.
6 You're The One That I Want
John Travolta & Olivia Newton-John
7 Relax
Frankie Goes To Hollywood
8 She Loves You
The Beatles
9 Unchained Melody
Robson Green & Jerome Flynn
10 Mary's Boy Child – Oh My Lord
Boney M.

England 1952 –2002. The Official UK Charts Company (OCC)

SINGLE RECORD. The biggest selling single until now is "Candle in the Wind" by Elton John and Bernie Taupin (lyrics). Originally released as a single from Goodbye Yellow Brick Road in 1973, the lyrics were about Marilyn Monroe. The tragic death of John's friend Lady Diana in 1997 made him rerecord the song, replacing the words "Goodbye Norma Jean" with "Goodbye England's rose". According to Wikipedia – The Free Encyclopedia, the single sold a staggering 33 million copies worldwide. All proceeds went to charity.

If there is any truth to the famous words of the architect Ludwig Mies van der Rohe that "God is in the details", this home could be mistaken for a temple. Inhabited by an author, it bears clear signs of a person who never stops reflecting or rearranging. Decorating is an art form, and here it is taken to artistic heights. Items designed by famous interior decorators find improvement in this well-appointed 56 m^2 cottage. An open question confronts the viewer: Why not?

THE DECORATOR ☞

MAKE AN ENTRANCE

"I never found the companion that was so companionable as solitude."

Henry David Thoreau

"Why shouldn't I look at my dearest treasure – at all the beauty that is mine, all my very own?"

A Doll's House (act 3), by Henrik Ibsen

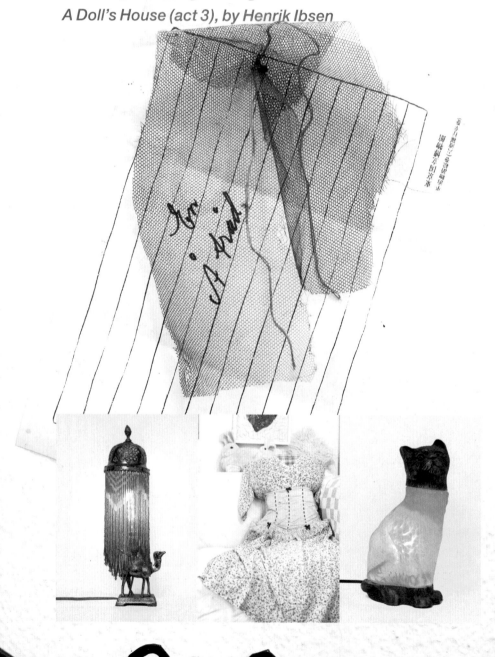

TV ROOM

CROWDED HOUSE. Though solitude is chosen, it's nice to have friends over from time to time. The library acts as a guest room, with no shortage of bedtime stories.

ROOM FOR IMPROVEMENT. Who decides when a design is final? The owner does in this home – and by the way, it is never final. Why let imagination rest?

BEDDED IN

"Too much of a good thing can be wonderful."

Mae West

KITCHEN-SINK
REALISM

For years we have been fed with pictures of ascetic, almost antiseptic kitchens. In her freedom from interference, the owner of this home takes on an opposite view. The kitchen has grown or overgrown with utensils, memorabilia and kitchen appliances into a secret system, known only to one person. Let's see now... where's the stove again... I'm sure I saw it this morning...

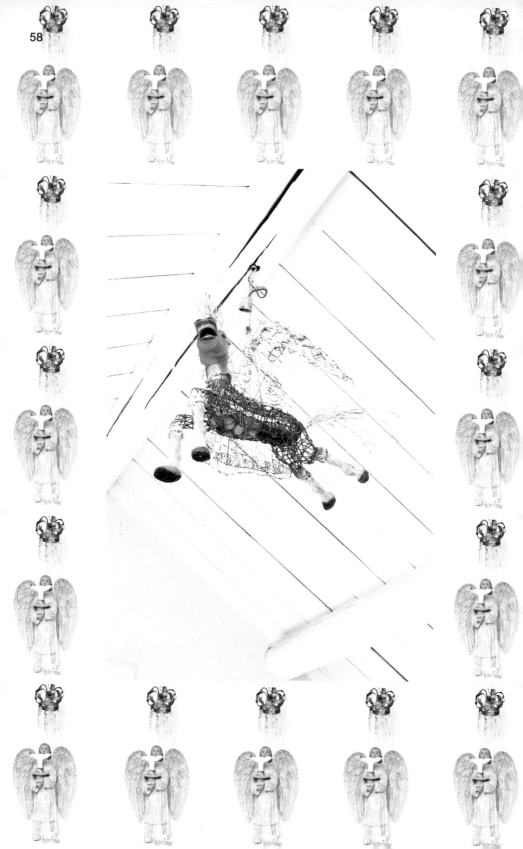

God is in the details

Films for singles

Breakfast at Tiffany's
Pippi Longstocking
Batman – The Beginning
The French Lieutenant's Woman
Dracula
Single White Female
Risky Business
Psycho
The Sweetest Thing
Down with Love

Reading for singles

Going Solo Roald Dahl
Solo Susan Fox Rogers
How to Be Alone Jonathan Franzen
I am What I am Jim Davis
Hard Rain Barry Eisler
Steppenwolf Hermann Hesse
A Room of One's Own Virginia Woolf
Living Alone and Loving It Barbara Feldon
Singular Pleasures Harry Mathews
Your Erroneous Zones Wayne W. Dyer
One Hundred Years of Solitude Gabriel García Márquez

SINGLE MALT. According to the Stockholm Single Malt Society, a 50-year-old Springbank is the best single malt you can drink. The downside is that it is priceless and impossible to find.

re:construction#5

Plants are wonderfully useful in decoration. And why use vases when you probably have a collection of shoes and boots lying around? Arrange them in whatever

fashion you like. Use plastic bags filled with soil for the
plants, and old glass jars for the flowers – in case you
want to reuse your shoes again.

When seeking peace of mind, many find comfort in nature. Some spend their holidays tenting in the wilds to draw energy from sleeping under the open sky. Here we have tried to capture the spirit of nature in an open-plan solution in an old greenhouse. Plants have a unique ability to clear the air.

They are also regarded by scientists as healers. Some claim they cure headaches and skin problems, and generally make us feel better. So living out of doors can only be good for us.

Step inside and experience the outside!

THE CULTIVATOR ☞

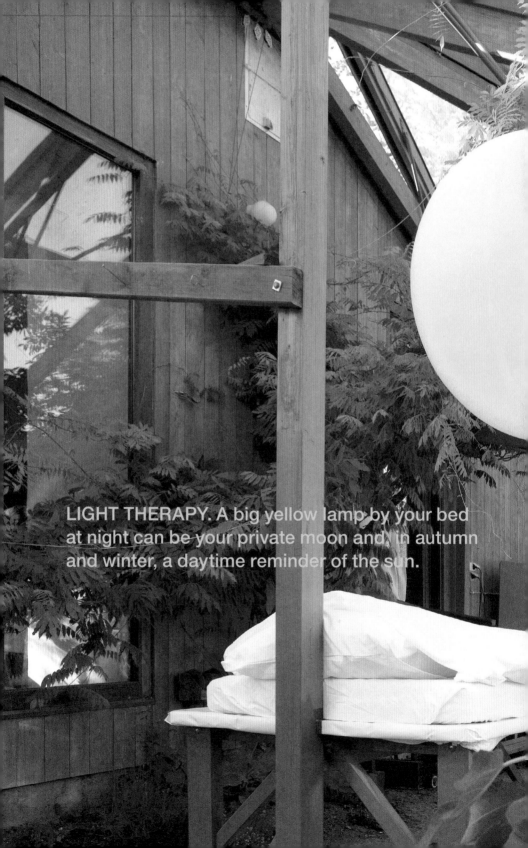

LIGHT THERAPY. A big yellow lamp by your bed at night can be your private moon and, in autumn and winter, a daytime reminder of the sun.

"I've made an odd discovery.
Every time I talk to a savant I
feel quite sure that happiness
is no longer a possibility. Yet
when I talk with my gardener,
I'm convinced of the opposite."

Bertrand Russell

SHOWER IN THE JUNGLE

PHOTOSYNTHESIS. Almost all living things depend on the energy produced by photosynthesis. Photosynthesis also produces much of the Earth's oxygen. It is fair to say photo-synthesis is vital to life on Earth.

"Tea tempers the spirit, harmonizes the mind, dispels lassitude and relieves fatigue, awakens the thought and prevents drowsiness"

Lu Yu
The Classic Art of Tea

HERE COMES THE SUN

GREENHOUSE EFFECT. One of the positive effects of gardening is the soothing and relaxing influence it has on the mind. It is also extremely good exercise, and we all know the importance of exercise to good health. One way to achieving a healthy lifestyle is to grow your own food. You don't even need a garden, a balcony will do. And the bonus is that it all

"HOW LOVELY
YELLOW IS!
IT STANDS
FOR THE SUN."

Vincent van Gogh

To brother Theo, 13 August 1888

"Spend some time
alone every day."

Dalai Lama XIV

PRICELESS APRON

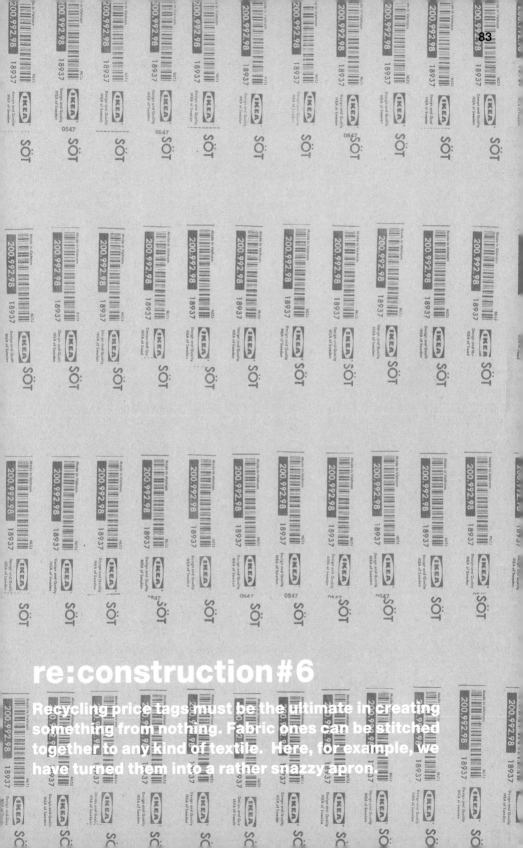

re:construction#6

Recycling price tags must be the ultimate in creating something from nothing. Fabric ones can be stitched together to any kind of textile. Here, for example, we have turned them into a rather snazzy apron.

re:construction#7

It might take a rainy afternoon and some swearing, but the result is awesome. Simple plastic straws can be hung using wire in this elegant shape. Keep away from pets!

re:construction#8

No home should lack superglue! It allows you to repair things, and it challenges your creative powers. Why buy models made by others when you can design your own mobile. The key word is EXPERIMENT! Or would you rather be glued to the TV?

What is it about the 1970s? As soon as one revival passes, another generation discovers the music, the colours, the fashion, the television programs. For some the decade was a time of freedom and political awareness. For others it was a cool period of great bands and fantastic design. And for others still, it simply never

went away. The following pages show a 125 m² ter-
raced house, that feels almost as if time stood still
somewhere around 1975. Or, as one of the icons of late
1970s, J.R. Ewing, put it: "Anything worth having is
worth going for – all the way."

THE TIME BANDIT 👉

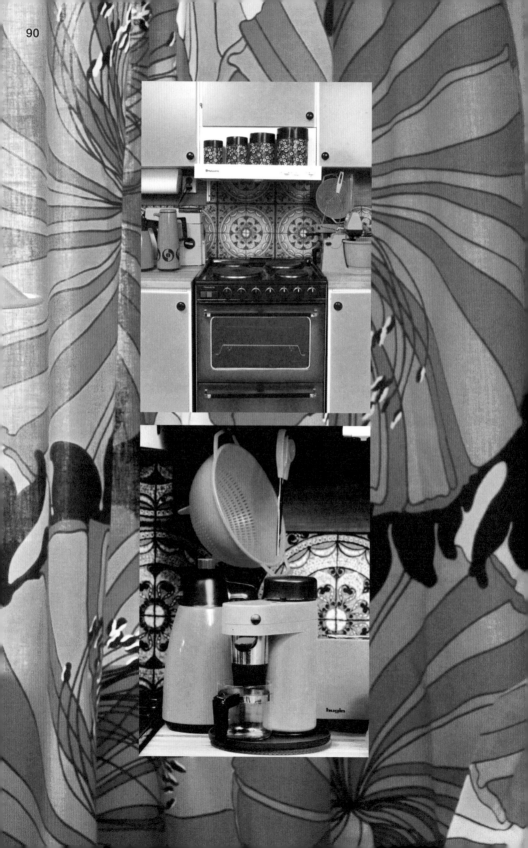

MATERIAL WORLD. The oil crisis of the mid-seventies brought a new element to our lives: Saving energy. We learned to block out the draughts, turn off the lights and install off-peak central heating. Paradoxically, there is probably no other decade that also brought us so many synthetic, oil-based materials.

SMURFIN' USA. Like the rest of the seventies, Smurfs are as popular as ever. Created by the late Peyo, Pierre Culliford, their popularity exploded when Smurfomania hit the U.S. Kids collected the Smurf figurines by the millions. And speaking of millions, if you happen to have an original Astro Smurf in mint condition, it could be worth a fortune.

"There is no business like Smurfbusiness", according to the official website.

CLEAN FUN. If you live the 1970s dream to its fullest, you may have to accept domestic appliances that are slightly less than state-of-the-art, like this vintage vacuum cleaner. On the other hand, it doesn't cost much to equip your home with an avocado-coloured cooker, bright orange coffee-maker and teak T.V. set.

"When the moon is in the Seventh House
And Jupiter aligns with Mars
Then peace will guide the planets
And love will steer the stars

This is the dawning of the age of Aquarius"

Aquarius, from the film Hair, 1979

THE BEDROOM

DO-IT-YOURSELF. In the 1970s the DIY market exploded. IKEA opened its first warehouse outside Scandinavia in the Zurich area in 1973. Plastic furniture was in its prime. The only trouble was that the furniture industry had no previous experience in plastic. To manufacture the chair SKOPA, IKEA had to turn to a supplier of plastic buckets and bowls. Maybe that's why it's named SKOPA, the Swedish word for scoop.

SINGLES BAR. What could better illustrate the seventies than the archetype of the time, the private bar? Not only did they drink frequently in the American television series broadcasted throughout the world, but many of the classic recipes date from this epoch. In 1976, the potent Long Island Iced Tea was invented by a bartender at the Oak Beach Inn of Hampton Bays (Long Island). The recipe includes equal portions of gin, vodka, rum, tequila and triple sec (Cointreau). Add some freshly squeezed lemon juice and a splash of Cola to a tealike colour. Yummy!

re:construction#9

Hide what you don't want to look at inside something visually interesting. All you need is a long belt – the sort truckers use to secure cargo – and a collection of different storage units. Tighten the belt and you have made a personal storage tower, as well as a great conversation piece.

NOTE. Take care how you stack the storage units to create a stable solution that won't tip over.

CONVERSATION PIECE

re:construction#10

Find out if H.C. Andersen was right, that a real princess will feel a pea right through twenty mattresses and twenty eider-down beds. Build your own "Princess and the pea"-bed out of simple soft rugs.

Put a pea under the bottom rug and try to sleep.

ARE YOU A PRINCESS?

For some, living solo means being able to live with animals, which a resident other might be allergic to. Here our host is a graphic designer who lives with her dogs on a converted steamer. However, the ship is safely docked so the dogs go ashore to answer the call of nature. The ship offers 80 m² of living space over three decks, and has been meticulously renovated and improved.

Welcome aboard, but take off your shoes first.

THE DOGMATIC 👉

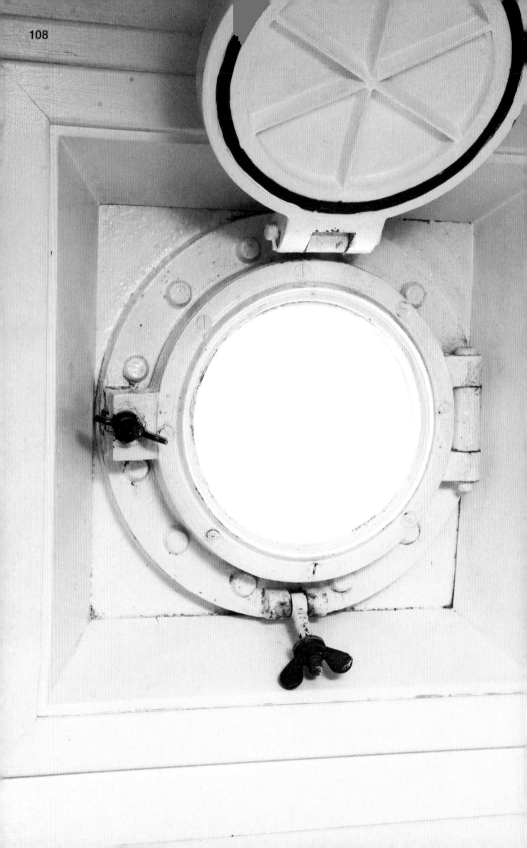

King
SAFETY MATCHES

KING OF DOGS. King Charles II (1630–85), king of England, Scotland and Ireland, loved dogs, hence the breed called the Cavalier King Charles Spaniel. The king was so fond of his dogs he took them everywhere with him, even aboard his naval vessels – to the annoyance of the sailors, because the dogs soiled the decks. It led to a series of unsolved disappearances of His Majesty's dogs.

TRICK OF THE TAIL. Bright red tails have been discreetly chosen for hooks in the galley.

HOT DOGS. The dogs on this ship are more than spoilt, admits the owner. They even celebrate birthdays. It must be close to doggy-heaven to get an entire curtain of sausages as a birthday present.

DECKED. The constant movement must be expected when living on a boat. Although it does not suit everyone, it is the best natural tranquilizer there is, say those who love being slowly rocked to sleep by the waves.

DREAM ON, DREAMER. If you are familiar with dogs you know they moan, growl, twitch and wag their tails when they sleep. These involuntary body gestures are not unlike how humans sleep and lead us to conclude that dogs dream! Sadly, dogs can't tell us their dreams. We must assume they dream about everyday life as humans do, eating, playing or being scratched behind the ear. There is evidence they have nightmares, too. Maybe about the Hound of the Baskervilles.

"**Whoever said you can't buy happiness forgot little puppies.**"

Gene Hill

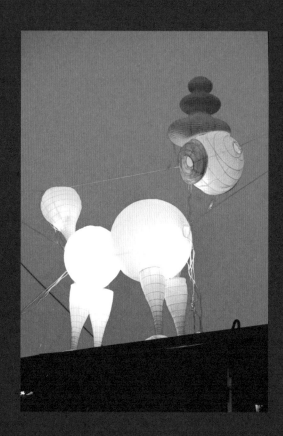

WAG THE DOG. The old steamer has a canine installation installed atop the bridge. Rice-paper lamps have been put together to resemble the body of a large hound. When the night breezes blow, it moves in the wind, just as if the tail were wagging the dog.

re:construction#11

String up your little friends – on a shoelace or whatever you have at hand. Make a whole curtain and you'll have quite a hanging. Not recommended for people with cats or dogs.

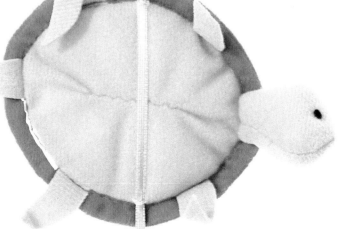

ANIMAL NIGHTLIFE

re:construction#12

Avoid nightmares and sleep with the lights on. This lamp, made of the cutest creatures of the night, will bore all the scary monsters under your bed.

NOTE: When making a lamp with flammable materials, make sure to take the proper precautions.

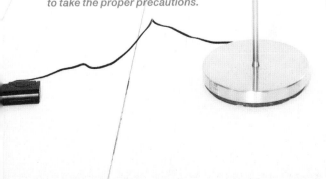

Danish designer Verner Panton (1926–98) played a key role in defining the colour schemes which were so popular during the sixties and seventies. His unique organic forms are more popular than ever. They are sought after by collectors all over the world, featured in exhibitions and interior magazines, and beloved of celebrities. Lenny Kravitz's home is full of Panton designs.

Here we meet another musician who has filled his home and studio with the works of the Danish designer. A 150 m² turn-of-the-century apartment, which underlines the importance of using designer objects for real purposes rather than viewing them as untouchable investments.

THE PANTOMANIAC 🖙

PANTOMINE. Without even knowing who had designed it, the owner of this home fell instantly in love with a lamp he had seen in a design shop, and bought it straightaway. It turned out to be a VP-Globe, by Verner Panton.

Shortly after he went to a Panton-exhibition and suddenly there was no turning back. Six years later the result is on display on these pages. A home dedicated to the Danish designer. The VP-Globe 40 is still in production, made out of transparent acrylic lucite with five hollowed-out aluminium reflectors with coloured lacquer finish. The lamp can be seen on the opposite page, hanging from the ceiling.

CRYSTAL PALACE. If Panton were alive today, the owner of these lamps would love to ask him if they represented his take on the classic crystal chandelier. Anyhow, they are utterly ravishing.

SPECTRAL: Imagine recording sad songs in this environment.
Impossible. You cannot be melancholy in such vibrant sur-
roundings.

LIVING TOWER. The music was psychedelic, the politics were left-wing and the colours were Panton. In 1969, Verner Panton created Living Tower in tribute to the spirit of experiment and adventure that characterized the era. By the way, it is a chair.

IN THE STUDIO

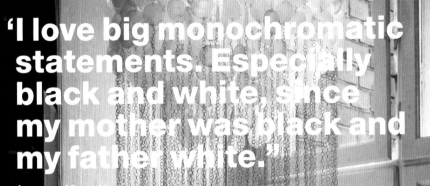

'I love big monochromatic statements. Especially black and white, since my mother was black and my father white."

Lenny Kravitz,
a musician with a passion for design in general and Verner Panton in particular, to the New York Times, 13 June 2008.

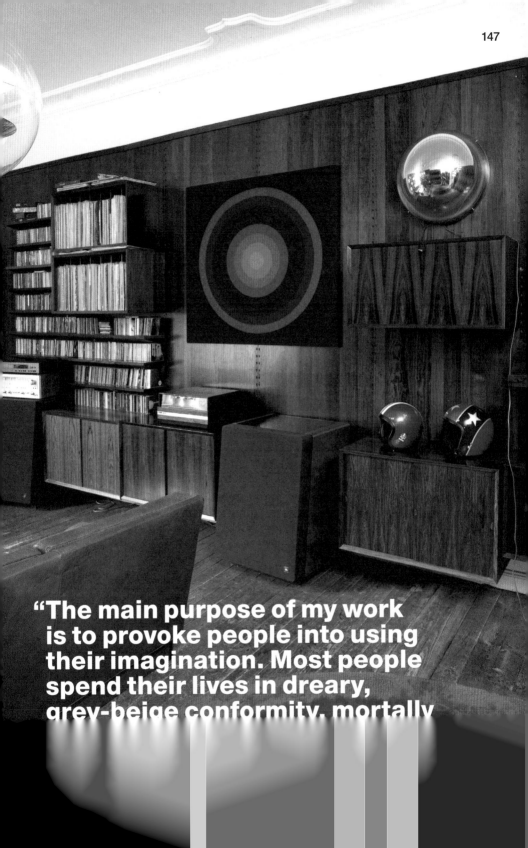

"The main purpose of my work
is to provoke people into using
their imagination. Most people
spend their lives in dreary,
grey-beige conformity, mortally

re:construction#13

A garment bag is probably the last thing you want to show off. But illuminated with a simple string of lights, it becomes a stylish wall lamp.

NOTE. When working with electric lights, check instructions thoroughly to see if the light can be covered.

The more the merrier.

re:construction#14

Lighting is an oft-forgotten interior detail. Attention paid to lighting can change a home completely. It doesn't have to cost a fortune. Many things can be brought to light, like these plastic colanders.

Buy some simple lights and check antique shops or your grandmother's attic. You might have a bright idea!

NOTE. When working with electric lights, check instructions thoroughly to see if the light can be covered.

SIEVE THE LIGHT

Here's proof that Life is the answer to so many questions starting with why. In this five-room apartment with a terrace, everything is possible. It's the ultimate playground of a grown-up who can't sit still, the extraordinary home of a textile artist who loves going completely over the top.

The decor is so full of surprises that you will need

to look very closely at the pictures to spot them all.
There are plenty of hand-made pieces as well as small
messages and tributes to those who wield a needle
and thread. The furniture is not simply furniture, but
veritable pieces of sculpture. Every corner of the home
sings a song with a clear message: It's great to be alive!

THE ARTIST ☞

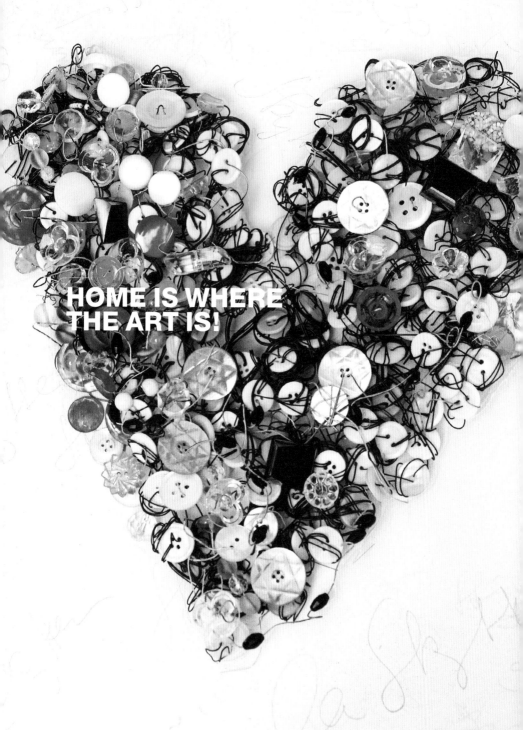

HOME IS WHERE
THE ART IS!

STATE OF THE ART. There's something profound about wool. Yet whim plays a role in creating artwork, as you can see looking at this cake/tower made from yarn and decorated with plastic mushrooms. The artist in this home started knitting when he was 4–5 years old.

FLAUNT IT! As children we were told to clear away our toys, make our beds and tidy our rooms. It can take a lifetime to get rid of those silly habits. Fight the shipshape blues. Don't clear the table; use it as an ideas palette.

oj
så lustigt
det kittlar
under
fötterna

får du inte
en känsla av
att det
kommer att
klarna upp
lite längre
fram på dagen

POSTERS. *Top:* Oh! It's tickling the soles of my feet.
Below: Don't you think it will brighten up later on?

LAVISHING COLOURS. Isn't it great to indulge in colours and textures? Odd pieces of textile in a multitude of colours cling to this outdoor table as colour splashes on an artist's palette.

Yes!

John Lennon went to an exhibition by the Japanese artist Yoko Ono and discovered that one of the pieces was a tall ladder to a small message written on the ceiling. He climbed the ladder and read the word: *Yes!* Many years later, he said that if the message had been *No*, he probably never would have met Yoko.

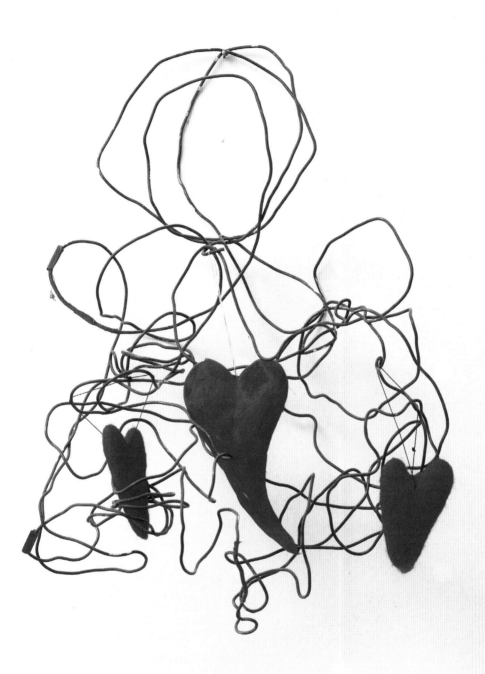

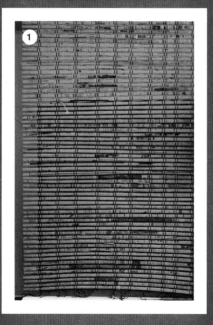

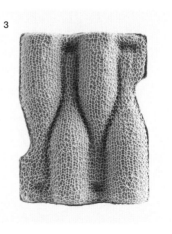

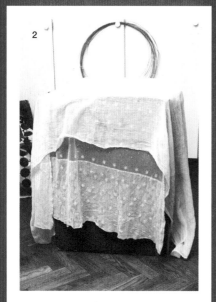

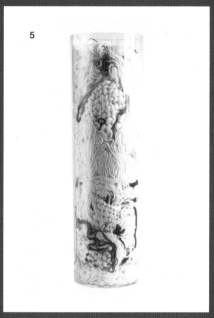

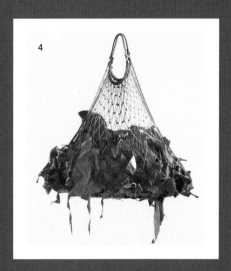

PRACTICAL JOKES. ❶ Blinds made out of old newspaper pages, tied together with black thread. Blinds could for instance be hung to hide messy bookshelves. ❷ Extremely simple storage solution. Cover and forget. ❸ Precious champagne bottles in a soft package. This textile composition is a work of art entitled *Fragile, fragile.* ❹ Net bag inspired by naval storage. Sailors used to get one bag for personal belongings to hang next to their hammock. ❺ Glass cylinders, sold as low-priced vases and great for displaying textiles you otherwise would hide in drawers and cupboards.

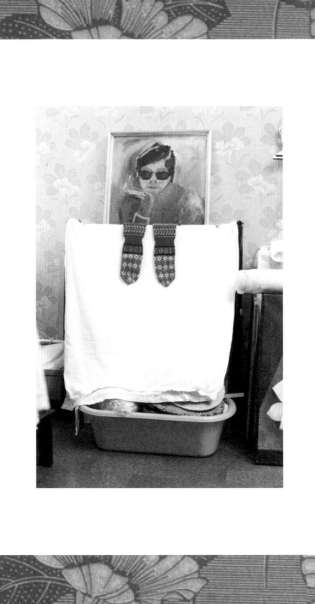

WHAT IS ART? Britannica Online defines it as "the use of skill and imagination in the creation of aesthetic objects, environments, or experiences that can be shared with others". Here is an example of how coincidence has evolved into art. Where does it start? Where does it end? It's in the eyes of the beholder.

DECK THE HALL. At Christmas, even hardcore minimalists can't keep from decorating. If you want to kick the habit, Christmas-decorate all year round!

re:construction#15

After paint, fabric is the easiest way to change the look of an interior. If you want to avoid the cost of an upholsterer, go DIY. Armed with a staple gun and a pair of scissors, before you know it you'll be on the path to changing your home.

SET THE TABLE

YULE-TIDY

re:construction#16

Recycling is fashionable, so why not go all the way and recycle the Christmas tree – or any old wooden skeleton you have lying about. Use it to hang kitchen utensils. It's inexpensive, unusual and ornamental.

Can you fall in love with a colour? Of course! Can you live with another person who hates that colour? No way. This single's paradise, measuring 65 m² plus kitchen, is PINK. It is an outstanding example of how you can mix and match your way to a personal expression, and a perfect reminder that we are individuals. Maybe we should strive harder to explore our individuality. French singer and artist Serge Gainsbourg once said, "White walls are for hospitals; I would go insane in a white room". He would have liked this flat.

THE PINK PANTHER ☞

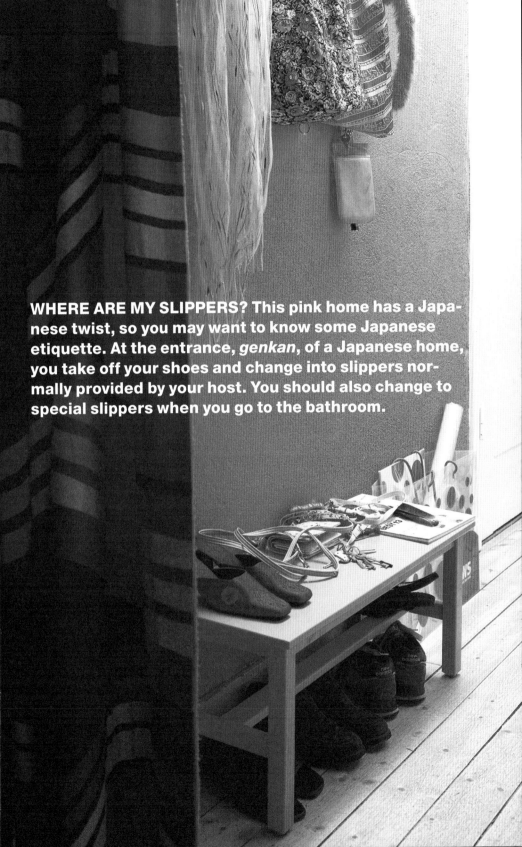

WHERE ARE MY SLIPPERS? This pink home has a Japanese twist, so you may want to know some Japanese etiquette. At the entrance, *genkan*, of a Japanese home, you take off your shoes and change into slippers normally provided by your host. You should also change to special slippers when you go to the bathroom.

LIVING ROOM, OFFICE, BEDROOM

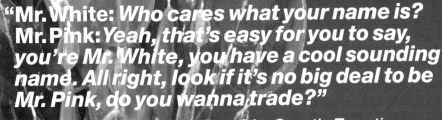

"**Mr. White:** *Who cares what your name is?*
Mr. Pink: *Yeah, that's easy for you to say, you're Mr. White, you have a cool sounding name. All right, look if it's no big deal to be Mr. Pink, do you wanna trade?*"

Dialogue from "Reservoir Dogs" by Quentin Tarantino

CHERRY BLOSSOM. No other flower in Japan is as celebrat-
ed and cherished as the cherry blossom.
   There are dozens of different cherry-tree varieties in Japan,
most of which bloom for just a couple days in spring. During
this time the celebration of *Hanami* takes place. Thousands
of people go to the parks to hold feasts under the trees and
watch the beautiful flowers together.

PINK VICTORY. *Maglia* [is the name] of the shirt or vest of the leader of [Giro d'Italia]. The [colour] is pink because the [sponsor], [La Gazzetta dello Sport], is a sports newspaper [printed on pink] paper.

HOUSE OF FUN. Scientists have long sought to understand why the people of Japan's Okinawa islands are among the longest-lived on the planet. One theory is that they have a positive attitude towards life. Bright colours are a way of showing positivity. Try it yourself!

FRAMED. Magazines have been accused of polluting our interior environments. If you like magazines, they get all over the place. Here's an idea. Stack them in a bookcase

with framed glass doors. Identify the most common colour on the magazine spines. Paint the frame that colour, and you have produced a new piece of furniture, instead of disorder.

PINK FLOYD? Not exactly. Meet Ken, Go and Junichi, three members of the popular Japanese band V6, one of many bands connected to the vast talent agency Johnny's.

The stars of Johnny's have millions of fans, predominantly female. One of them lives in this pad.

TOYS ARE LUSH. Redecorating a bathroom is less expensive than tearing it down and rebuilding. The world is full of fantastic plastic figures and hooks to lift the mood of a gloomy bathroom. Spice up an evening bathing by candlelight with a glass of cool pink champagne.

"What a lovely surprise to finally discover how unlonely being alone can be."

Ellen Burstyn